THE NEW GOURMET BABY COOKBOOK

150 FRESH, FUN & HEALTHY RECIPES

Kristi Riches
(Oscar's mum)

1663 LIBERTY DRIVE, SUITE 200
BLOOMINGTON, INDIANA 47403
(800) 839-8640
WWW.AUTHORHOUSE.COM

First published by AuthorHouse 12/08/05

ISBN: 1-4259-0138-7 (sc)

Printed in the United States of America
Bloomington, Indiana

This book is printed on acid-free paper.

Never give babies under 12 months salt.

Dedication

To my son, Oscar

Thank you for being my
best and worst critic

INTRODUCTION

As like any other mum, I wanted to give my son Oscar the very best I could and to offer him as much variation as possible with his diet.

Baby's nutrition in their first year has a great influence on their tastes, choices & social future.

As a professional cook and restaurant owner for 10 years I have a strong passion for cooking with the freshest of ingredients and eating them! I wanted Oscar to experience from a very young age all the aromas & tastes of great fresh food.

So with Oscar's mealtimes I started. Most of the recipes in this book are quick and easy, full of great fresh flavours and most of all additive and preservative free.

What is even better is that half of these recipes are used for our dinner parties and feeding the rest of the family.

In recipes I have allowed seasoning, this is optional and minimal.

NEVER give babies under 1 year salt.

The biggest inspiration for this book is my son Oscar, who is also my biggest critic so only the good recipes made it! Oscar was born with special needs and it was believed that he would never be able to eat orally. So when at 4 months Oscar had his feeding tube removed and started to eat orally, that was it , I could not wait to start cooking for him. Oscar's first solid food was pureed apricot & he loved it.

This spurred me on to cook a lot more un-restrained for Oscar and to look at marrying up fresh ingredients that I maybe would have not cooked together. Oscar eats almost anything from chicken fajitas to chilli beef.

When Oscar turned 2yrs old he asserted his opinion at meal times more so I listened & came up with more different meals to excite him. There is over a million meal combinations out there, but it is easy to fall into a routine, especially when grocery shopping, as it becomes habit to put the same regular items in your shopping basket. So I always try to put something new in my basket that I have not used before or in a long time.

Some helpful hints when feeding your child, is always allow them to feel in control and never force your baby to eat anything they are refusing, evening if it is something you know they usually love, this will create a negative impression. When a child refuses to eat they are using the only control they have over you, so listen and ask them why.

There is nothing like the anxiety created in a mum when a child keeps on refusing to eat. This I have been through, gained grey hairs over, but with the help of Oscar's feeding therapist have learnt to overcome the feeling of making Oscar eat or feeling frustrated and in return Oscar now eats more as he knows that I am listening to him and he feels in control and relaxed.

It is amazing, looking back how easy it was, and with Oscar's response and progress as the proof, I highly recommend staying calm.

I also resort to tactics! Sometimes I will put a small bottle of fresh fruit and carrot juice in the fridge, I make sure Oscar knows that I am looking after the bottle for a favorite super hero and label the bottle accordingly.

As always Oscar will ask if he can have some, I respond with the lines, I am not sure, it may have super powers and I don't know if I should give you some, what do you think Oscar.

You've guessed it, he always say's yes !!!

When asking your child what they want for a meal, instead of just asking, offer them a choice of two, so that they have to choose one, this always removes the chances of an upset, as they have to choose one, so once again they feel in control of their choice.

List of Receipes

NEVER GIVE SALT TO BABIES UNDER 12 MONTHS.

ONION MARMALADE RISOTTO

65g arborio rice
1 small red onion, finely chopped
1 small knob of butter or teaspoon olive oil
1 tsp brown sugar
270ml chicken or vegetable stock
(fresh stock recipe on page 29/64)

Heat a saucepan, gently melt the butter or oil, add the finely chopped onion, cook on a medium heat for 7-10 minutes until very soft & transparent in colour. Add the sugar & keep stirring until you have lovely caramelized onions. Add the Arborio rice & stir for one minute, pour in the entire stock, simmer gently stirring occasionally more frequent towards the end, when all the stock has been absorbed.

FRUITY TUTTI RISOTTO

65g arborio rice
1 small red onion finely chopped
1 knob of butter
4 strawberries
1 apricot
270ml vegetable stock
(fresh stock recipe on page 29)

Heat a saucepan, gently melt the butter add the onion, cook on a medium heat for 7-10 minutes until very soft, add the Arborio rice & keep stirring for 1 minute. Pour in all the stock & simmer gently stirring occasionally & more at the end when all the stock has been absorbed. Take off the heat and stir in half the fruit & cover with a lid for 3 minutes, use the remaining fruit to decorate the top & serve.

STUFFED SWEET ONIONS

2 medium white onions
(1 finely chopped)
1 teaspoon brown sugar
1 tsp butter
1 rasher of un-smoked bacon
1 tbsp cream cheese
sprig of thyme

Heat a saucepan, gently melt the butter & fry the chopped onion until soft then add the sugar. When caramelized take of the heat & mix in the cream cheese & leave to one side.

Take the whole onion, peel & slice of the top, gently pull out the middle, starting in the centre. Stuff the onion with the caramelized mixture. Grill the bacon & wrap around the onion using a sprig of fresh thyme to skewer the bacon to the onion. Wrap loosely in tin foil & bake for 10-15 minutes in a moderate heat.

CREAMY CHEESE &
SPINACH MUSHROOMS

2 mushrooms (remove stalks)
1 tsp butter
small handful of fresh spinach
50ml double cream (or full fat milk)
2oz mild cheddar cheese
1oz fresh parmesan
pinch of nutmeg

Melt the butter & add the sliced mushrooms cook until just soft, take of the heat & stir in the spinach. Put in an oven proof dish ready to top with the cheese sauce.

To make the sauce, heat the cream with the nutmeg until almost simmering do not let the cream boil, take off the heat & add the cheddar cheese & stir well. Pour over the mushrooms & top with parmesan.

Place under the grill until browned off.

COCONUT CHEESE BALLS

125g cream cheese
50g breadcrumbs
50g coconut
1tsp mild curry powder (optional)

Mix the cheese, breadcrumbs & curry powder into a stiff paste, gently divide into balls & roll in the coconut, chill & serve on sticks or loose.

Why not add a pureed peach dip?

CHEESEY FINGERS

finger slices of edam
finger slices of mild cheddar
dollop of cream cheese
dollop of raspberry jam
dollop of marmalade

Mix the cream cheese & raspberry jam together & place
in a ramekin in the centre of a plate, arrange the finger
slices of cheese around the plate, maybe stacking them
high like a tower, put the marmalade on the side.

Serve with plenty of kitchen roll!

FRUITY MOZZARELLA

fresh chunky slices of
pineapple
peach
banana
kiwi
strawberries
mozzarella cheese
sprigs of mint

Standing the fruit on its side, layer alternative fruits, then every 3rd or 4th use mozzarella & so on dress with sprigs of mint.

Why not puree some strawberries in a little syrup & drizzle over the fruit.

FRUITY COTTAGE CHEESE

4oz cottage cheese
2 fresh strawberries
or peach
1 slice of wholemeal toast

Mash the strawberries or peach with a fork, add to the cottage cheese, fold in, do not over stir as to keep a ripple effect.

Cut the toast into fingers & top with the fruity cottage cheese.

Cottage cheese too sour, then use cream cheese instead.

SPEEDI VEG FINGERS & FRUITY MAYO DIPS

fingers of
raw carrot
celery
baby corns
cucumber
cauliflower

Prepare all the vegetable fingers by washing, scrubbing or peeling, slice into thin fingers, but stiff enough to hold the dip.

Why not cut into stars, squares & triangles?

For the fruity mayo dip, blend or crush the fruits of your choice & gently mix into the mayo.

Blend the mayo with you choice of fruit.

Best fruity mayo from Oscar's choice is apricot mayo or raspberry mayo.

POTATO WEDGES & DIP

large jacket potato
crème fraiche
cream cheese
chives
strawberry jam

Scrub the jacket potato, boil whole in simmering water until three quarters soft, drain & leave to go completely cold.

Roll the potato on its side & slice in half, lay the flat side on the board and cut in half length ways again & again. This gives you your wedges.

Toss the wedges in some seasoned olive oil with rosemary.

Pre-heat your oven to gas mark 7, bake the wedges for approx 20-25 minutes.

Mix the crème fraiche, cream cheese & chives together & top with strawberry jam.

LEMONADE OR
BEER BATTERED VEG

plain flour
egg
milk
non-alcoholic beer or lemonade
honey
pepper
cauliflower
broccoli
baby corns

Mix the flour, pepper, egg, lemonade, honey & milk into a smooth batter, part steam the cauliflower & broccoli when cool toss the vegetables in seasoned flour, then dip into the batter, repeat & gently fry until golden in colour, drain well & allow to cool a little before serving.

Don't forget to add a tasty dip.

FRUIT PATE

1 tbsp cream cheese
1 small banana
1 tsp brown sugar
1 drop vanilla essence
buttered toast fingers

Slice the banana & sprinkle over the sugar, pre-heat a non-stick pan & cook the banana until caramelized.

Half mash the banana with the cream cheese & vanilla essence & press firmly into a mould or ramekin & chill.

Serve a wedge of fruity pate with the toasted fingers.

CHEESE MOUSSE

2 eggs separated
beat the yolks & whip stiff the whites
50g cheddar cheese
1 tsp mild mustard
pinch nutmeg
150ml double cream whipped stiff
fruit slices to garnish

Beat the eggs yolks, mix in the cheddar cheese, mustard & nutmeg then fold in the whipped cream followed by the stiff egg whites.

Pour into dishes & garnish with your choice of fruit slices, chill until serving.

BEANS ON CRUMBS

125g cream cheese
1 slice of bread for breadcrumbs
1 tsp butter (optional)
1 tin baked beans
1 tbsp ketchup

Heat the beans gently & let simmer so that they are very soft & thick, mix in the cream cheese & ketchup. Take off the heat.

In a separate pan melt the butter & toast off the bread crumbs.

Serve the beans topped with toasted crumbs.

Why not add a dusting of parmesan & grill?

CHEDDAR CHEESE SOUP

1 tsp butter
100g grated mature cheddar
1 onion
1 potato finely diced
900ml vegetable stock
70ml double cream
pinch of mustard powder

Gently melt the butter, fry the onion & potato for 3 minutes, add the mustard powder, seasoning & stock. Cook for ½ hour simmering gently. Pour through a sieve & bring back up to simmering point then add the cream stir well & add the cheese, keep stirring until smooth, then serve.

Why not try this as a sauce,
add four cheeses & pour over chicken?

OSCAR'S GREAT GRANNYS
SUPER HERO SOUP

1 tin tomato soup
1 cooked sausage
1 onion diced
1 slice ham
1 tin baked beans
2 tbsp ketchup
1 tin chop tomatoes
1 tsp butter

Chop all the ingredients & put in a large stock pot, add
the soup, beans, butter & tomatoes, simmer & serve
with lots of bread & butter fingers.

OSCAR'S WILD RAREBIT

225g cheddar
25g butter
1tsp mustard powder
45ml ale (non-alcoholic)
seasoning
pinch cayenne pepper (optional)
4 slices warm toast

Gently heat the ale, butter, mustard, seasoning & cayenne pepper when warm add the cheese & stir constantly until thick & smooth. Spread generously on the toast & grill until browned off.

ASPARAGUS CHEESES TOASTIES

4 spears of asparagus
1 tsp butter
4oz cream cheese
2 slices of brown toast

Melt the butter, steam the asparagus until cooked, add to the melted butter, toss & then blend. Mix with the cream cheese.

Spread either on top of the toasted fingers or in between two slices of bread & toast.

For extra flavour brush some melted butter over the toast.

MINI CROSTINI'S

French stick or ciabatta sliced
whole garlic clove
fresh tomato de-seeded & finely chopped
4oz mild cheese
fresh finely chopped coriander

Toast both sides of the bread finger slices in a dry pan, rub the garlic clove over the bread. Top with slices of cheese & finely chopped tomato, grill until the cheese starts to melt approx 2-3 minutes & garnish with coriander

Why not top with onion or orange marmalade?

MUSHROOM FINGERS

4 fresh mushrooms
1 tbsp butter
pinch black pepper
100ml double cream (or half fat)
½ garlic clove
pinch nutmeg
2 slices of toast fingers

Gently melt the butter, add the sliced mushrooms, garlic, pepper & nutmeg. When soft add the cream & bring up to a very gentle simmer, do not boil. Turn off the heat & leave to cool, blend well into a thick paste. Top high on the toasted fingers.

CREAMED CHICKEN PATE STUFFED MINI PITTA'S

4oz chicken breast
2 tbsp of cream cheese
50ml double or half fat cream
1 small red onion
1 tsp white sugar
1 tsp butter
1 small red pepper
pinch of salt & pepper (optional)
mini pitta breads

Melt the butter & gently fry the onion when soft add the sugar stir until caramelized, add the chicken & cook well, half way through add the red peppers & season. Now add the cream & bring to almost a simmer do not let the cream boil. Take off the heat & leave to cool slightly then blend in to a smooth paste, add the cheese & stir well, there should be enough heat left to melt the cheese. Spread onto toasted fingers or stuff mini pitta breads.

GO BANANAS & PEANUTS SANDWICH

two slices of bread
1 banana sliced
peanut butter smooth
1 knob of butter

Spread one slice of bread with peanut butter & the other slice with banana slices, press together & spread the butter on the OUTSIDE of the sandwich.

Heat a non-stick frying pan to a medium high heat & fry both sides of the sandwich turning only once until both sides are crisp.

This makes the sandwich really tasty with a gooey sweet sticky filling.

OSCAR'S ROYAL SOFT SCRAMBLED EGGS

1 egg
100ml double cream
pinch nutmeg
2 tbsp cream cheese

In a saucepan heat the cream & nutmeg to simmering point add the cream cheese & stir until fully mixed. Gently fork the egg & add to the cream, keep stirring for at least 30 seconds then take off the heat, keep stirring until cooked, the heat of the saucepan will keep the egg cooking.

Serve alone or with toasted fingers.

Why not with a dollop of tomato ketchup?

KING OF CREPES

1 egg
pinch of seasoning
50g mild cheddar

Heat a small non-stick frying pan to a medium high heat with a dash of oil. Gently fork the egg, season & mix in the cheese. Pour into the frying pan and DO NOT TOUCH for 30 seconds!!

Lift up one side of the frying pan & with a spoon drag the crepe to the other side, so that the uncooked egg runs down on to the saucepan.

Leave for approx 15 seconds & repeat.

Take off the heat & fold over each side into the middle, roll over and leave in the pan for 1 minute then slide onto a plate.

POSH FINGER FUN

Take toasted fingers, melba toast, mini pitta's, crackers biscuits or puff pastry bases & top with the following suggestions of toppings.

MUSTARD CREAMED CHEESE

Just mix cream cheese & mild mustard.

TOMATO CORIANDER ORANGE SALSA

Blend a tin of tomatoes, sprigs of coriander, peeled orange, dash of lime, salt & tomato puree.

VERY BERRIED CREAM SPREAD

Just mix cream cheese with mixed berry jams.

STUFFED CHERRY TOMATOES

Cut off the top & scoop out the middle with the handle end of a teaspoon, stuff with orange marmalade & bake for 10 minutes.

Why not stuff with cream cheese & coriander?

VEGETABLE STOCK

1 onion chopped
1 carrot chopped
1 celery broken
2 cloves garlic crushed
1 courgette chopped
1 tbsp butter
1 bay leaf
1 sprig of thyme
½ lemon
½ tsp mustard powder
pinch salt
pink & black peppercorns
2 pints of hot water

Gently melt the butter in a large stock pot, fry off the onion, garlic & celery until soft, but no change in colour, add the rest of the ingredients & bring to a simmer for at least 1 hour. Cool & pour off through a strainer.

Alternatively you can blend the whole stock pot & have a more textured stock.

ORANGE CARROTS

2 carrots
400ml fresh orange juice
100ml water

Bring to the boil the orange & water mixed together add the chopped carrots & simmer until almost all the liquid has gone, at this point stay with the pan until 95% of the liquid is gone.

Mash with a fork or blend.

APRICOT CARROTS

1 tin apricots
6 carrots
200ml orange juice
400ml water
pinch of nutmeg

Bring the orange juice & water to a boil, add the tin of apricots in their juice, nutmeg & chopped carrots, simmer until 95% of all the liquid has evaporated then blend or mash.

Why not change the fruit to Mango,
Peaches or Prunes?

CHICKEN STOCK
BRAISED CARROTS

2 carrots
400ml chicken stock
100ml orange juice

Bring the chicken stock & water to the boil add the chopped carrots & simmer until nearly all the liquid has evaporated.

Stay with the pan until 95% of the stock has gone.

Mash with a fork or blend.

ORANGE SWEET POTATO
& CARROT

1 sweet potato
2 carrots
500ml orange juice
200ml water

Bring the orange juice & water to the boil and add the diced potato & carrots.

Simmer until nearly all the liquid has gone, stay with the pan until 95% has evaporated.

Mash or blend.

HONEY ROASTED PARSNIPS

1 large parsnip
2 tbsp honey or golden syrup
olive oil

Peel & slice the parsnip into long fingers, part boil until soft in centre. Heat the olive oil in a non-stick frying pan toss in the parsnips & crisp all sides, drain off any excess oil, return pan to the heat & add the honey keep tossing the parsnips until completely caramelized.

CHEESEY PARSNIP POTATO CAKES

1 parsnip
1 potato
1tbsp plain flour
1 egg yolk
50g mature cheese grated
seasoning
pinch of nutmeg
1 tsp butter melted
olive oil

Grate the potato & parsnip, lay on thick paper roll & squeeze out all liquid.

In a large bowl mix the grated potato & parsnip, cheese, nutmeg, salt, pepper & melted butter, mix well add the egg yolk & mix thoroughly. Form into patties, dust very lightly with flour & pan fry on a slow medium heat until crisp & golden on both sides.

SWEET ORANGE MASH

4 large potatoes
2 sweet potatoes
1 tsp sugar
1 orange
25g butter
salt & pepper

Bring to the boil a large pan of water, season add the peeled & quartered potatoes, cook for 5 minutes then add the sweet potatoes.

Cook until soft in the centre, drain well & return to the pan.

Peel & roughly chop the orange, sprinkle with sugar & mash into the potatoes, adding the butter & seasoning Why not top with your favorite cheese & bake.

SWEET POTATO & SWEDE BAKE

1 small swede
4 sweet potatoes
25g butter
seasoning
50g to 100g parmesan grated

Bring to the boil a large pan of water, season add the peeled & chopped swede, cook for 5 minutes then add the sweet potato. Cook until soft in the centre. Drain well & return to the empty pan. Mash, add the butter & seasoning then stir in the parmesan leaving ¼ for topping.

Place in a oven proof dish & top with the remaining parmesan, brown off under the grill.

SWEET & SOUR MASH

2 large potatoes
2 sweet potatoes
½ lemon juice
½ lime juice
1 tbsp white sugar
1 tbsp brown sugar
50g butter melted

Boil the potatoes until soft & mash. In a separate bowl mix the lemon & lime juice, sugars & melted butter, add this to the mash & stir in well. Place in an oven proof dish & bake on gas mark 7 for 20 minutes for a fluffy finish.

TENNESSEE MASH

6 sweet potatoes
1 red pepper finely chopped
½ lemon juice
1 tsp white sugar
1 tsp brown sugar
25g melted butter
50ml maple syrup
(for the grown ups use bourbon whiskey)!!

Boil & mash the potatoes, in a separate bowl mix the red pepper, lemon juice, sugars, butter & maple syrup together add to the mash mix well, pour into a oven proof dish & bake for 20 minutes on gas mark 7.

FIVE * STAR * VEGETABLE * MASH

1 bunch broccoli
1 courgette
1 large handful fresh spinach
1 clove garlic
1 red pepper
1 onion
2 potatoes
2 sweet potatoes
25g butter
50ml double cream (optional)
100g cream cheese

Peel & dice the potatoes, add to a pan of boiling water with the clove of garlic. Boil & mash. Meanwhile cut the broccoli & courgette into bite size pieces & steam just for a couple of minutes as they will cook very quickly. When cooked take off the heat & add the spinach to welt.

Gently melt the butter & fry the diced onion & red pepper until soft. Mix everything into the mash with the cream cheese & seasoning. Add the cream for a richer taste & texture if you wish.

JAMMY MASH

4 large potatoes
2 carrots
3 tbsp strawberry jam
25g butter
salt
pepper

Bring a large saucepan to the boil & add the chopped potatoes & carrots. Mash with the butter & season. Either stir in the strawberry jam or fold in to have a ripple effect.

Try with other jams or even lemon curd!

MARMALADE MASH

4 large potatoes
2 tbsp fine marmalade
50g butter
salt
pepper

Boil & mash the potatoes with the butter then season.
Either top the mash with the marmalade, or fold in to
give a ripple effect

CARAMELIZED BANANA MASH

2 potatoes
1 banana
1 tbsp brown sugar
25g butter (twice)

Boil & mash the potato with 25g of butter.

With the rest of the butter gently melt in a pan & fry the sliced banana until warm all the way through, sprinkle with sugar & caramelize.

Gently fold the banana pieces into the mash.

CARIBBEAN HAPPY MASH

4 sweet potatoes
2 slices pineapple
½ lime juice
1 banana
25g desiccated coconut
25g butter
50g cream cheese

Boil & mash the potato with the butter, lime juice, cream cheese & coconut. Roughly chop the pineapple & banana & mix into the mash.

THREE CHEESE MASH

4 potatoes
25g butter
50g gruyere cheese
50g emmental cheese
50g parmesan
seasoning

Boil & mash the potato with the butter & seasoning, grate the cheese & fold into the mash, for more texture some of the cheese can be cut into small chunks, this will give hidden pockets of cheese to find.

Place the mash in an oven proof dish, sprinkle on the parmesan & bake for 20-30 minutes or if still piping hot just brown off under the grill.

PRUNE MASH

4 potatoes
1 tin of apricots
6 de-stoned prunes
25g butter
100g cream cheese
salt
pepper

Boil & mash the potato with the butter & season. Finely dice the apricots & prunes, mix into the mash with the cream cheese.

If you want to loosen up the mash save some of the juice from the apricots.

SWEET GARLIC & GRAPE MASH

2 potatoes
25g butter
salt
pepper
1 clove of garlic
1 tsp sugar
10 red grapes halved

Bring a large pan of water to the boil add the garlic & potatoes, mash with butter & seasoning.

Toss the grapes in sugar & fold into the mash.

PARMESAN POTATO DISCO

2 large potatoes
25g butter
seasoning
50g gruyere cheese grated
50g parmesan grated
1 crushed garlic clove
salt
pepper
nutmeg
50ml double cream

Finely slice the peeled potatoes. In a mixing bowl put the potatoes, season with salt, pepper & nutmeg.

Heat the double cream with the butter & crushed garlic, do not boil.

Pour over the potatoes & mix well so that every slice is coated. Drain off any excess liquid & toss in the grated cheeses, keeping a little back for topping. Bake in an oven proof dish for 45 minutes on gas mark 6.

CAULIFLOWER CHEESE

1 small cauliflower
100g gruyere cheese grated
100g mild cheddar grated
50g parmesan grated
pinch nutmeg
1 tsp mustard powder
300ml double cream
1 knob butter

Steam the cauliflower & leave to drain well. Heat the cream & butter gently, add the mustard powder & nutmeg. When the cream is at just simmering point take off the heat & stir in the gruyere & cheddar, keep stirring until smooth. Put the cauliflower in an oven proof dish & pour over the sauce top with parmesan & brown off under the grill.

CHEESE & APPLE FONDUE

1 onion finely diced
25g butter
1 tsp sugar
100g gruyere cheese grated
50g emmental cheese grated
50ml orange juice
50 ml apple juice
2 apples
bread sticks

Melt the butter & gently fry the onion until soft, sprinkle on the sugar & caramelize, pour in the orange & apple juice & bring to a simmer. Add the cheese & stir thoroughly until smooth.

Peel & slice the apples into fingers, place with the breadsticks for dipping into the fruity fondue.

STUFFED CHEESE DUMPLINGS

100g plain flour
50g suet
30ml chicken stock
50g mature cheddar grated
salt
pepper

Put the flour, suet, cheese & seasoning in a bowl mix well, add the stock. Form into soft balls & bake for 15-20 minutes.

Why not add to the Persian one pot chicken?

HIDDEN TREASURE BREAD

500g bread mix
water
100g mild cheddar
2 fresh tomatoes diced
2 slices pineapple diced
pepper

Make the bread mix according the instructions. Portion off into small balls half the size of a tennis ball. Stretch out the ball with the heel of your hand & stuff in some of each of the fillings & form back into a ball.

Leave to prove & bake for approx 15-20 minutes. Allow to cool slightly before serving or just serve cold.

APRICOT ONION STUFFED TOMATOES

1 beef tomato
1 onion
1 tsp sugar
50ml water
1 apricot

Finely dice the onion & panfry until soft add the sugar caramelize, add the diced apricots & water, then reduce down to a chutney texture.

Take the top of the tomato, scoop out all the insides, fill with the onion & apricot marmalade.

Bake in a moderate oven for 20 minutes.

RED PEPPER JAM STUFFED ONION

1 medium white onion
1 red pepper
1 tbsp strawberry jam
1 tsp sugar
100ml orange juice
1 garlic clove
1 small red onion
fresh coriander
1 slice un-smoked back bacon

Dice the red onion, pepper & garlic, gently fry in 25g butter until soft, sprinkle on the sugar & caramelize. Add the strawberry jam & orange juice, reduce down to a thick chunky stage.

Cut the top of the onion, peel & trim the roots only, scoop out ½ the centre, these sections should just lift out from the centre first with a little encouragement. Stuff with the mix, top with coriander & wrap the grilled bacon slice around the outside & secure with a sprig of thyme or cocktails stick, bake for 20 minutes.

HONEY MUSTARD STICKY VEGETABLES

1 bunch broccoli
1 carrot
1 courgette
1 apple
50ml tbsp honey

Steam the carrot fingers first until ¾ cooked, then add the broccoli & courgette. Peel the apple & cut into segments.

Heat a deep pan & bring the honey up to a simmer, toss in all the vegetables & apple in to the honey & caramelize.

OSCAR'S WILD MUSHROOM
& SPINACH CHEESE

100g wild mushrooms (regular ok)
25g butter
100g fresh spinach
100g gruyere cheese
50g parmesan
100ml double cream
pepper

Melt the butter gently & pan fry the mushrooms until soft add the spinach, season & take off the heat. In a separate pan heat the cream & bring up to a simmering point, don't allow to boil, add the gruyere cheese & stir until smooth. Place the mushrooms in a dish, pour over the sauce, top with parmesan & brown off under a hot grill.

ORANGE BACON

2 rashers un-smoked bacon
1 red pepper
1 orange
1 onion
1 clove garlic
50g spinach
25g butter
salt & pepper
fresh coriander

Finely chop all the vegetables, orange & bacon, melt the butter in a large pan & gently cook all the vegetables & bacon, when just soft add the seasoning & coriander toss & serve.

CREAMY CHEESE VEGETABLES

1 small cauliflower
1 bunch broccoli
1 onion
1 clove garlic
25g butter
salt & pepper
nutmeg
400ml double cream
200g mild cheddar grated
100g parmesan grated

Steam the cauliflower & broccoli until just soft drain & leave to stand. In a saucepan melt the butter, fry the onion & garlic until soft, season & add the nutmeg. Stir in the cream & bring up to a simmer, take off the heat & stir in the cheese until you have a smooth sauce.

Put vegetables in a dish & pour over the cheese sauce, top with parmesan & bake.

ORANGE BRAISED RICE

100g basmati rice
salt
pepper
1 pint of orange juice
1 pint of chicken stock
4 sprigs of coriander
tbsp parsley

Wash the rice in a large bowl of running water until clear, leave soaking for ½ hour. Bring to the boil the chicken stock & orange juice, drain the rice & add. Cook until the rice is soft drain well, season with all the herbs.

FRUITY RICE

100g basmati rice
salt
pepper
2 pints of chicken stock
½ tin apricots
½ tin peaches

Wash the rice in running water & leave soaking for ½ hour if you can.

Bring the chicken stock to boil & add the rice, when cooked drain well & season. Finely dice the fruit & mix in with the rice.

Why not try different fruits?

MANGO & BANANA RICE

1 mango diced
1 banana sliced
2 pints of chicken stock
100g basmati rice

Wash the rice in running water & then leave to soak for half an hour. Bring to boil the chicken stock & add the drained rice, cook & drain.

Add the diced mango & banana to the rice

Why not use apricots & mango instead.

COCONUT & PAPAYA
ORANGE BRAISED RICE

100g basmati rice
1 pint of orange juice
1 pint chicken stock
50g grated coconut
1 papaya diced

Wash the rice in running water & leave to soak for ½ hour. Bring the chicken stock & orange to boil and add the drained rice. When cooked drain & add the diced papaya & coconut.

CHEESE & ONION RICE

100g basmati rice
2 pints chicken stock
1 onion
1 tsp sugar
25g butter
50g cheddar cheese cubed
50g gruyere cheese cubed
salt & pepper

Wash the rice in running water & leave to soak for ½ hour. Bring to the boil the chicken stock & add the rice, cook & drain. Melt the butter & gently fry the onion until soft, add the sugar & caramelize. Season the rice, stir in the caramelized onion & cubed cheese.

CHICKEN STOCK

1 chicken chopped
5 pints water
pinch peppercorns
2 bay leaves
2 onions chopped
2 leeks chopped
2 cloves garlic
1 carrot chopped
1 celery chopped
sprig of thyme
salt

In a large saucepan melt the butter & gently soften the vegetables, do not allow to colour, add the garlic, bay leaf & peppercorns. Pour in the water, drop in the chicken & sprig of thyme. Bring to the boil & simmer for 3 hours. Any film or froth needs to be skimmed off. Drain through a sieve & cool.

Freeze any left over stock for later use.

MAMA MIA CHICKEN

chicken breast
1 beef tomato
1 red onion
1 green pepper
1 clove garlic
25g butter
fresh coriander
pepper
salt
50g parmesan grated

Lay cling film on top of the chicken breast & bash with a rolling pin till almost the same thickness all over.

Melt the butter & pan fry the finely diced onion, garlic, red pepper & seasoning. Chop the tomato & coriander, mix in with the pan fried vegetables. Grill the chicken breast, remove & top with the tomato salsa, sprinkle with parmesan cheese, grill until browned

BELLA CLUCK CLUCK

chicken breast
1 small courgette
1 onion
1 clove garlic
1 red pepper
25g butter
300ml double cream
pinch nutmeg
100g mild cheddar
1 portion pasta shells

Gently melt the butter & fry the finely diced onion, garlic & red pepper until soft, add the sliced courgette & chicken, cook then add the cream & nutmeg, bring up to simmering, add the cheese & stir well, pour over the cooked pasta shells & serve.

CREAMY BACON CHICKEN

1 chicken breast
2 rashers un-smoked bacon
50g mild cheddar
50g red Leicester
50g parmesan
pinch black pepper
pinch nutmeg
200ml double cream

Cover the chicken with cling film & bash with a rolling pin so that the chicken is the same thickness all over. Wrap the bacon around the chicken & grill.

Heat the cream, simmering, add the pepper & grated cheeses, stirring until smooth then pour over the chicken & serve.

MUSHROOM STUFFED CHICKEN

1 chicken breast
4 mushrooms
1 tsp butter
1 clove garlic
1 handful fresh spinach
(Why not use apricots instead of spinach?)

Cover the chicken breast with cling film & bash with a rolling pin so that the chicken is the same thickness all over. Butterfly the breast.

Melt the butter slowly & pan fry the finely sliced garlic & mushrooms until soft, take off the heat & stir in the spinach.

Stuff one side of the chicken breast & fold over the other side to create the pocket. You can blend this stuffing if you want.

Rub the breast with butter then wrap in tin foil & bake for approx 20 minutes.

HONEY CHICKEN

1 chicken breast
1 tsp butter
2 tbsp honey

Cover the breast in cling film & bash with a rolling pin so that the chicken is level all over.

Gently melt the butter & pan fry the chicken breast gently, you can also cut the chicken into finger strips, when just cooked, turn up the heat & add the honey & caramelize

APRICOT CHICKEN

1 chicken breast
1 tin apricots blended
50 ml orange juice
1 tsp sugar

Slice the chicken into fingers & grill, in a saucepan heat the apricots, orange & sugar. Reduce down to required consistency. Serve in a dipping bowl with the chicken fingers.

Why not top a whole piece of chicken with the apricot sauce.

APRICOT & CREAM
CHEESE CHICKEN

1 chicken breast
1 tin apricots
200g cream cheese

Slice the chicken into bites size pieces or fingers &
grill. Blend the apricots & heat in a saucepan, mix
in the cream cheese & take off the heat. Serve in a
dipping bowl with the chicken pieces for dipping.

HERBIE CHICKEN

1 chicken breast
15g butter
1 clove garlic
1 beef tomato
1 sprig of thyme
3 sprigs coriander
salt

Mix the butter with the finely diced garlic, half of the coriander & thyme. Finely dice the tomato & mix with the remaining herbs.

Rub the chicken all over the herb butter & grill.

Serve with the finely diced tomato & herbs on top & season.

OLIVE & BASIL CHICKEN

1 chicken breast
8 fresh basil leaves
2 olives
3 rashers of bacon
15g butter

Make a small slice in the side of the chicken, stuff with half the butter, olives & basil leaves. Seal the opening with a cocktail stick. Rub the rest of the butter on the chicken, lay the rest of the basil leaves on top of the chicken & wrap the bacon around the chicken. Griddle slowly until cooked.

HONEY & MUSTARD CHICKEN

1 chicken breast
3 tbsp honey
1 tsp course grain mild mustard

Mix the mustard & honey together, baste some on the chicken & griddle. In a saucepan heat the rest of the sauce & pour over the chicken.

Hint, slice the chicken into fingers

COCONUT FRUITY CHICKEN

1 chicken breast
200ml coconut cream
2 pineapple slices
½ tin mango slices
50g desiccated coconut
1 red pepper
1 clove garlic
olive oil

Finely dice the garlic, pepper & chicken, heat the oil & pan fry until ¾ cooked, add the chopped pineapple & mango, cook for 3 minutes add the coconut cream, heat through, sprinkle on the coconut & serve.

LEMON CHEESE CHICKEN

1 chicken breast
½ lemon sliced
½ lemon squeezed
100g cream cheese
30ml milk
pinch nutmeg
pepper
chives

Heat the milk & cream cheese together in a pan, add the nutmeg & pepper stir until smooth, keep stirring & add the lemon juice. Grill one side of the chicken, remove from the grill & turn over, place the lemon slices on the chicken & put back under the grill, top with the lemon cheese sauce & chives.

TENNESSEE CHICKEN

1 chicken breast
for the BBQ sauce
200ml ketchup
50ml honey
1 tbsp Tabasco
1 tsp garlic powder
1 tsp white wine vinegar
3oz brown sugar
10 dashes Worcestershire sauce
1 green pepper finely chopped
1 onion finely chopped
water

Mix all the sauce ingredients & bring the mixture to the boil. Reduce heat & simmer for 1 hour. Allow to cool & blend. Add the amount of water you require for the thickness of the sauce. Grill the chicken (optional slice into fingers) & smother with the Tennessee BBQ sauce.

STINKY CHICKEN

1 chicken breast
1 tbsp mild blue cheese
100g cream cheese
30ml milk

Mix the milk & cheeses together & warm through gently in a saucepan. Griddle the chicken & then slice into fingers, either top the chicken with the stinky sauce or serve as a dipping sauce.

Why not add Apricots or Strawberries to this?

CHOCOLATE CHICKEN

1 chicken breast
large plain cooking chocolate

Melt the chocolate in a bowl over a gently simmering pan of water. Slice the chicken into fingers & grill. Allow to cool & dip into the chocolate, place on a cooling rack to dry & then repeat the process. Stack high on the plate & serve cold.

MAPLE CHICKEN

1 chicken breast
2 rashers un-smoked bacon
50ml maple syrup

Wrap the chicken breast with the bacon & griddle, heat the maple syrup for approx 20-30 seconds, be careful as this gets very hot. Pour over the chicken on the serving plate.

For an added zing you could pan fry the bacon with onions, garlic & peppers, then pile this high on the chicken & drizzle with the maple syrup.

PERSIAN ONE POT CHICKEN

1 chicken breast
1 green pepper chopped
1 onion diced
1 clove garlic
2 pints chicken stock
1 potato diced
1 sweet potato diced
1 tbsp butter
olive oil
200g basmati rice

Heat the oil in a large saucepan, gently fry the chicken, onion, garlic & pepper until soft, add the butter & potatoes, stir until the butter melts. Add the stock & bring up to a simmer for 30 minutes, add the rice & cover with a lid, cook for 10 minutes, take off the heat & leave to stand for 5 minutes, 95% of the stock should be absorbed by the rice, if not just take the lid off & reduce down a little or add some red lentils.

SIMPLE LEMON BUTTER CHICKEN

1 chicken breast
50g butter
1 lemon unwaxed
pepper
nutmeg
chives
parsley

Mix the butter, nutmeg, pepper & herbs together. Grate the rind of the lemon & add to the butter, take three slices of the lemon & then squeeze the rest. Mix half of the butter with half of the lemon juice. Score the chicken diagonal across the top & rub the lemon butter mix into the groves, top with the three slices of lemon & grill. As serving on a plate place the remainder of the butter in two or three dots on top.

CHICKEN BACON BEAN CASSEROLE

1 chicken breast
4 rashers bacon
1 celery stick
1 carrot chopped
1 onion chopped
1 clove garlic chopped
1 tin mixed beans
2 pints chicken stock
1 tbsp butter
2 potatoes roughly chopped
fresh parsley
sprig thyme
olive oil

Heat the oil & gently fry the onion, garlic, bacon, chicken & celery, until soft then add the butter & stir in the carrot, potato, beans & herbs. Add the stock & cook for one & a half hours on a slow heat with the lid on. If you like your casserole thicker reduce down.

CHICKEN FRIED CHICKEN

1 chicken breast
3 tsp paprika
3 tsp pepper
3 tsp garlic salt
3 tsp white pepper
200g plain flour
300ml single cream
1 egg

Mix all the dry ingredients, take 3 tbsp & put in a dish, in the bowl create a well in the centre, crack in the egg & pour in the cream. Whisk until completely smooth. Dust the chicken in the dry flour mix, dip in the batter, back into the flour mix & back into the batter. Deep fry for approx 4 minutes.

BEEF STOCK

8oz beef trimmings
(left overs from your butcher)
3lb beef bones
2 onions halved
4 carrots chopped
3 sticks celery halved
4 tomatoes quartered
1 leek chopped
3 whole skin on garlic cloves
1 bay leaf
sprig of thyme
salt
6 pints water

This takes time & effort, but is so worth it. Take a roasting tray add the onions & dash of water, cook for 1 hour on medium heat. Place the onions in a stock pot. Using the same tray roast the carrots, celery, tomatoes, leek & garlic for 20 minutes, then add to the stock pot. If you have a double oven you can do this at the same time as each other.

BEEF STOCK cont...

Roast the bones & beef trimmings on a high heat for 30 minutes then add to the stock pot along with the bay leaf, thyme, salt & water. Bring to the boil & simmer for as long as 6 hours if possible. If the stock reduces down just add a little more water. If you wish to make a sauce from this stock, after 5 hours let the stock reduce all the way down. If a film appears on the stock just skim off & discard.

Hint check the flavour along the way so as not to spoil.

JAMMY BURGER

100g beef mince
100g pork mince
2 prunes pureed
2 tbsp raspberry jam
1 onion chopped
1 garlic chopped
olive oil
50g breadcrumbs
1 egg yolk (optional if needed)
toasted buns
cheese slices (optional)

Heat the oil & gently fry the onion & garlic until soft, add to a mixing bowl & stir in the mince, prunes & breadcrumbs, then add the jam, if the mixture is very stiff add the egg yolk to loosen slightly. Form into patties or little burger balls & griddle. Serve in a toasted bun with your choice of toppings, tommy k & oven fries go down best.

MANGO & BANANA BURGER

½ mango mashed
½ banana mashed
100g beef mince
100g pork mince
50g breadcrumbs
50g parmesan cheese grated

Mix all the ingredients together in a large bowl, form into patties or balls, dust with seasoned flour if needed & griddle.

Serve in a toasted bun with tommy k & fresh homemade potato wedges.

BIG KAHUNA BURGER

100g beef mince
50g mild cheddar grated
pinch salt & pepper
4 prunes pureed
1 slice pineapple
burger cheese
toasted bun

Mix all the ingredients together & form into patties or balls dust with flour if needed & griddle. Serve in a toasted bun with the pineapple slice & cheese as toppings

Why not serve with a fruit smoothie?

SWEET ONION BURGER

100g lamb mince
100g beef mince
3 tbsp ketchup
2 tbsp sugar
dash Worcestershire sauce
1 onion chopped
olive oil
spring onion
slice of burger cheese
toasted bun

Heat the oil & gently fry the onion, until soft, sprinkle with sugar & caramelize. Mix in a bowl with the rest of the ingredients & form into patties or balls & dust with seasoned flour if needed & griddle. Serve in a toasted bun with spring onions, cheese & side of oven fries or wedges.

CHEESE STUFFED BURGER

100g beef mince
100g pork mince
50g breadcrumbs
25g parmesan
pinch salt & pepper
100g chunks of cheddar

Mix the mince, breadcrumbs, parmesan & seasoning, form into patties or balls & push a couple of the chunks of cheddar into the centre of each pattie. Dust with seasoned flour if needed & griddle. Can be served in a toasted bun with tommy k or as balls with a mango & apricot dip.

GROOVY DISCO BURGERS

100g beef mince
50g lamb mince
25g parmesan
25g coconut desiccated
1 slice pineapple puree
50g breadcrumbs

Mix all the ingredients together & form into patties, dust with flour if needed, griddle & serve in a toasted bun with tommy k. Do a double disco burger & serve with a cocktail umbrella through the bun to hold the burgers in place. Serve with ketchup mayo & fries.

CREAM CHEESE STIR FRY

4oz rump steak sliced in fingers
½ red pepper sliced
½ green pepper sliced
1 onion diced
fresh parsley
fresh chives
100g cream cheese

Heat a wok & brush with a little oil, fry the rump steak for one minute, add the peppers & onion, cook for a further one minute, add the cream cheese, stir well & serve garnished with the chives & parsley.

OSCAR'S SESAME STICKY FINGERS

4oz rump steak sliced
50ml maple syrup or honey
small handful sesame seeds

Heat a large non-stick pan & toast off the sesame seeds. Heat a wok & brush with oil & fry the steak for 1 minute, drizzle in the syrup, stir for 1 minute, add the toasted sesame seeds & serve.

Why not add slices of fruit or vegetables?

BLUE PINEAPPLE DIPPING STEAK

4 oz rump steak
½ pineapple pureed
50g mild blue cheese
2 tbsp sour cream
1 tbsp mayo
fresh chives
seasoning

Season & grill the steak & slice into fingers. In a bowl mix the pineapple & cheese, add a little of the sour cream & mayo to loosen until you have a dipping consistency, mix in the chives & put in a bowl for dipping & stack the steak fingers around the bowl.

MINTY STEAK

4oz rump steak
coriander
mint
parsley
thyme
olive oil
1 red pepper
1 clove garlic
seasoning
50g cream cheese

Heat the oil & sear the steak fingers until half cooked, add the peppers & garlic, stir for 1 minute, add all the herbs & stir. Add the cream cheese stirring well.

This dish can also be pureed & served as pate on toast fingers or stuffed into giant pasta shells.

STEAK & PRUNES

1 tin prunes pureed
8oz rump steak
1 onion chopped
1 clove garlic
1 tbsp butter

Melt the butter & fry the onion & garlic until soft, add the fine strips of steak. Cook ¾ way through, add the prunes, heat through & serve.

You can add a tbsp of crème fraiche or cream cheese to make more of a sauce & serve with spaghetti

STICKY ORANGE STEAK

4oz rump steak sliced
50ml orange juice
1 tbsp marmalade
1 onion diced
1 tsp sugar
olive oil

Heat the oil & fry the onion for 2 minutes, sprinkle with sugar & caramelize, add the orange juice & reduce down. Stir in the marmalade. Griddle the steak & top with the sauce.

You can blend this chutney for a smooth consistency.

GRAPE BRAISED STEAK

1 pint of beef stock
8oz diced braising beef
1 onion chopped
1 carrot chopped
2 potatoes chopped
1 garlic clove chopped
1 leek chopped
seasoning
thyme
parsley
1 bunch sweet red grapes
1 tbsp sugar
dash olive oil

Heat the oil in a large casserole dish & gently soften the onion, garlic, grapes & leeks. When soft add the sugar, stir until dissolved, add the carrot, potatoes & beef. Once the beef is sealed add the stock & seasoning, simmer & cook for 2 hours on a low heat. If stock to loose, leave lid off & reduce gravy down.

NEW YORK CORN BEEF HASH

1 large potato
1 tin premium corned beef
1 tbsp butter
seasoning

Finely dice the potato & break up the corned beef. Gently melt the butter & fry the potato for 4-5 minutes. Season & add the premium corned beef & cook until hot & serve.

COKE BBQ DIPPERS

8oz steak fingers
pepper
BBQ sauce
(recipe as follows)
50ml coke
4oz tomato ketchup
dash lemon juice
dash white wine vinegar
dash Worcestershire sauce
seasoning
1 tbsp butter

Melt the butter in a pan, add the ketchup, lemon juice, vinegar, Worcestershire sauce & coke, simmer until thick, add seasoning & chill before serving.

Dust the steak fingers in the pepper & grill, serve cold with your homemade coke BBQ sauce for dipping.

BRAISED PORK & APPLE

8oz pork fillet
seasoning
onion
garlic
large cooking apple sliced
350ml apple juice
olive oil

Finely slice the pork fillet & seal in the oil quickly, remove from the pan, brown off the onions with the garlic & apple then add the pork & apple juice. Cover & cook slowly for 1 hour. You should be left with a medium thick apple stock, if you feel the stock is too thin, turn up the heat & reduce down.

CREAMY CHEESEY PORK

4oz pork fillet
onion
1 tsp sugar
1 tbsp butter
200ml double cream
100g gruyere cheese grated
100g mild cheddar grated
pinch nutmeg

Gently melt the butter & soften the onions, add the sugar & caramelize, add the pork fillet & seal, place to one side. Heat the cream & bring up to a gentle simmer, add the cheese & nutmeg keep stirring until smooth & then take off the heat. Drizzle over the pork & serve.

Why not add slices of apple or potato?

CHEESE STUFFED PORK BURGERS

100g favorite cheese
200g pork mince
seasoning
1 apricot pureed
sage
thyme
coriander
50g fresh bread crumbs
1 egg yolk

In a large bowl mix thoroughly the mince with the seasoning, herbs, apricot & breadcrumbs. If the mixture feels to firm, add the egg yolk to loosen. Start to form the patties & press in some of the cheese into the pattie. Griddle & serve plain or in a toasted bun with cheese, tommy K and oven fries.

CHEESEY TOAD IN HOLE

1 lb prime pork sausages
125g mild cheddar cheese
250ml milk
1 tsp mustard powder
2 eggs
pinch salt
125g flour

Brown off the sausages in a pan, mix the flour with the salt & mustard powder, beat in the eggs & milk until you have a smooth batter consistency. Mix in the cheese, heat some oil in a oven proof dish add the sausages & batter, put straight back into the oven & cook on a moderated heat for 25-35 minutes.

SAUSAGE MASH & ONION GRAVY

2 sausages
2 sweet potatoes
2 potatoes
1 onion diced
1 onion finely diced
15g butter (twice)
3 tbsp brown sugar
400ml vegetable stock
(or apple juice)

Peel, dice & mash the potatoes with the butter & seasoning. Cook the sausages. Place a large mound of mash in the middle of the plate, cut the sausages in half & stick them in the mound, to look like a hedgehog!

THE ONION GRAVY

Melt the butter & fry the diced onion until very soft, blend into a puree, return to the pan & add the sliced onion & cook slowly until very lightly browned, add the sugar & caramelize. Add the vegetable stock or apple juice & reduce down until you have the thickness of gravy.

BLACKCURRANT & APRICOT LAMB

1 leg NZ lamb
1 tin apricots
3 cloves garlic skin on
tsp rosemary
tsp thyme
seasoning
1 carrot chopped
2 onions quartered
300ml blackcurrant cordial
2 pints water

Seal the lamb on a griddle, rub with salt & pepper, rosemary & thyme. Place in a large casserole dish with the onions, garlic, carrots & apricots. Mix the cordial with the water & pour over the lamb. Cover & cook on the hob on a low heat for 3 hours. Remove the lamb & garlic. Squeeze the garlic puree from the skins back into the stock & blend, reduce down to make the best ever gravy, slice the lamb into bite size fingers & serve with the gravy.

RASPBERRY BURGERS

100g lamb mince
4 tbsp raspberry jam
seasoning
50g breadcrumbs

Mix the lamb, jam, seasoning & breadcrumbs together
& form into patties or balls, griddle & serve in a toasted
bun with tommy k or more raspberry jam.

PEACH SALSA SPAGHETTI

1 peach finely chopped
6 fresh tomatoes diced
1 onion diced
1 clove garlic crushed
1 red pepper chopped
1 green pepper chopped
5 sprigs coriander
seasoning
spaghetti

Fry the onions & garlic, add the peppers & cook for a further 2 minutes, add the tomatoes peaches & seasoning cook for 5 minutes, then add the coriander & take off the heat. Leave chunky or blend. Cook & drain the spaghetti & mix into the salsa.

APRICOT & RASPBERRY SPAGHETTI

1 tin apricots chopped
10 raspberries
3tbsp raspberry jam
100ml cooked
spaghetti

Heat 200ml water, add half the apricots & the raspberry jam. Simmer until most 95% of the water has evaporated. Blend into a puree then add the rest of the apricots & raspberries. Cook & drain the spaghetti & mix into the sauce.

CREAMY GOURMET LASAGNE

100g fine beef mince
100g lamb mince
1 tbsp butter
8 fresh tomatoes crushed
2 tbsp tomato puree
1 onion diced
1 clove garlic crushed
pinch of oregano
parsley
seasoning

SPEEDI CHEESE SAUCE

1 onion diced
1 tbsp butter
400ml double cream
pinch nutmeg
pinch cloves
1 bay leaf
100g grated mild cheddar
50g parmesan for topping
PASTA
Box of uncooked lasagna sheets

Melt the butter in a large saucepan & soften the onion & garlic. Remove from the pan & fry the mince on a high heat & do not stir, when browned turn over & repeat. Remove from the pan. Now add the tomatoes, tomato puree, seasoning, herbs & cooked onions, cook for 5 minutes then add the mince, heat through, then take off the heat.

THE SAUCE

Melt the butter in a saucepan with the bay leaf, nutmeg & clove add the onion & soften. Remove the bay leaf, then sprinkle in the sugar & caramelize, add the cream & bring up to a simmer, take off the heat & add the cheese, stir until smooth.

THE PASTA

In a oven proof dish place some lasagna sheets on the base, top with the mince then pasta, then cheese sauce, repeat this to the top finishing with cheese sauce, top with the parmesan & oven bake for approx 30 minutes.

GOURMET BOLOGANSE

100g lamb mince
100g beef mince
1 tin tomatoes
1 tbsp tomato puree
1 onion
1 clove garlic
1 tbsp butter
pinch thyme
fresh parsley
seasoning
5 sprigs coriander
spaghetti
50g parmesan grated

Gently melt the butter in a large saucepan & soften the onion & garlic, add the thyme parsley, coriander, tomatoes & puree. Cook for 5 minutes. In a separate pan heat some oil & brown off the mince, season & drain, add to the sauce. Cook the spaghetti & serve topped with parmesan cheese.

SPANISH ORANGE SALSA SPAGHETTI

4 tomatoes diced
1 clove garlic chopped
1 onion diced
1 orange diced
3 sprigs coriander
1 tbsp butter
seasoning
100ml orange juice
½ red pepper diced
½ tin tomatoes
spaghetti

Melt the butter & soften the onion, garlic, pepper, tomatoes & orange. Add the orange juice & reduce, blend the tin of tomatoes, season & add with the coriander.

Cook & drain the spaghetti & toss in the sauce.

SPEEDY HERBIE PASTA

1 onion chopped
1 tsp sugar
1 tbsp butter
1 clove garlic chopped
4 tomatoes chopped
8 sprigs coriander
thyme
parsley
basil
seasoning
pasta shells

Melt the butter & soften the onion, garlic & tomatoes, add the sugar & caramelize, mix in the chopped herbs, season & take off the heat. Cook & drain the pasta shells & mix with the sauce.

Why not add some fruit?

CHICKEN PASTA BAKE

4 oz chicken breast
1 onion diced
1 clove garlic diced
3 tbsp cream cheese
150ml double cream
seasoning
nutmeg
1 portion pasta shapes
125g cheddar grated

Gently soften the onion & garlic, add the chicken & cook through, add the cream cheese, cream, seasoning & nutmeg, bring up to a simmer & stir in the cheddar until smooth. Cook & drain the pasta & mix with the sauce, brown off under the grill.

OSCAR'S SHARK BAIT

2oz fresh tuna sliced
2oz rump steak sliced
3 tbsp flour
seasoning
pinch nutmeg
pinch mustard powder
1 egg yolk beaten

Season the flour with nutmeg, mustard, salt & pepper. Dip the fish & steak slices in the egg then the flour, repeat & lightly fry.

BACON WRAPPED FISH FINGERS

4 slices sweetcure bacon
4 oz white fish
100g breadcrumbs
50g flour
seasoning
fresh coriander
fresh parsley
1 egg yolk

Season the flour & mix in the finely chopped coriander, parsley & breadcrumbs. Wrap the bacon around fingers of fish & dip in the egg yolk then into the flour, repeat. Oven bake for 15-20 minutes.

You can reverse the method & coat the fish fingers in the herb flour & then wrap in bacon.

COCONUT & CHOCOLATE
FISH FINGERS

50g grated coconut
50g plain cooking chocolate
4oz white fish sliced into fingers

Griddle the fish fingers & let cool. Gently melt the chocolate in a bowl over simmering water. Dip the fish fingers into the chocolate & then roll in the coconut, for a really thick texture, repeat, cool in the fridge before serving.

HOOK LINE & SINKER DIPPERS

2oz white fish sliced
2oz fresh tuna sliced
100g breadcrumbs
25g flour
seasoning
thyme
rosemary
1 egg yolk

SINKER DIP

1 tbsp mayo
1 tsp tomato ketchup

Blend the herbs, seasoning, flour & breadcrumbs, dip the fingers into the egg, then the breadcrumbs, repeat & grill for 5-7 minutes. Mix the mayo & ketchup together & serve stacked high with the dip in the middle.

BANANA & MANGO LIME TUNA

1 banana sliced
1 mango sliced
1 tsp sugar
1 fresh lime squeezed
6oz fresh tuna
(can use any fish)

Heat a large non-stick pan & caramelize the banana slices with the sugar, add the mango, heat through, then squeeze in the lime juice & take off the heat. Griddle the tuna & top with the caramelized fruit. For a different texture blend the fruit & top the tuna.

SNAPPY DRESSER

6oz fillet red snapper
½ fresh lime juice
3 slices of lime
½ mango sliced
1 tbsp brown sugar
seasoning
tin foil pouch

Make a tin foil pouch, season the snapper & place in the pouch, add the mango, sugar, lime slices & juice. Seal the pouch & either BBQ for 5 minutes or oven bake or steam for 5-7 minutes.

PIRATES TREASURE PIE

8oz white fish
4 tbsp cream cheese
200ml double cream
150g cheddar
1 sweet potato
1 potato
1 onion diced
1 clove garlic chopped
1 tbsp butter
pinch nutmeg
seasoning

Melt the butter, soften the onion & garlic, season & add nutmeg, add the cream cheese & cream bring up to a simmer & stir in the ¾ of the cheese. Boil & mash the potatoes with butter & season. Gently pan fry the fish, place in an oven proof dish, pour over the cheese sauce & top with the mash, sprinkle the remaining cheese & bake for 25-30 minutes.

SALMON & TUNA MASH

2oz tinned tuna
2oz tinned salmon
2 sweet potatoes
1 potato
1 onion diced
1 clove garlic crushed
1 red pepper chopped
25g butter twice
parsley
dill (optional)

Gently soften the butter & fry the onion, pepper & garlic, add the tuna & salmon, heat through & add the herbs. Boil & mash the potatoes with the butter, cream cheese & seasoning. Gently fold in the fish.

You could pipe the mash as tots & bake or make fish patties or balls.

POACHED HOLLANDAISE FISH

6oz of any fish
200ml milk
1tsp butter
parsley
coriander
seasoning
one poached egg (optional)

HOLLANDAISE SAUCE

3 egg yolks
½ juice lemon
20ml water
1 tsp butter

In a roasting tray pour in milk & butter, drop in the fish, cover with foil & poach in the oven for 20 minutes.

In a bowl over simmering water place all the hollandaise sauce ingredients & keep softly whisking until you have a light smooth thick sauce, take off the heat & season. Take out the fish & top with finely chopped herbs, top with poached egg & drizzle over the hollandaise sauce.

PIRATES CANNON BALLS

1 small onion diced
1 tbsp butter
1 tsp sugar
1 clove garlic diced
1 rasher sweetcure bacon
200g cream cheese
2oz white fish

Gently melt the butter & soften the onion & garlic, add the sugar & caramelize. Stir in the chopped bacon & fish, cook for 2 minutes, take of the heat & allow to cool. Stir in the cream cheese & form into balls & serve cold.

Serve with toasted fingers or mini pitta breads.

BANANA CRÈME BRULEE

1 banana pureed
vanilla pod or extract
100ml double cream
2 egg yolks
1 tsp brown sugar

In a glass bowl over a pan of boiling water infuse the cream with the vanilla, whisk in the egg yolks gently & keep stirring until thick.

In a serving dish or ramekin layer some slices of banana pour in half the custard, some more banana & top off with the remaining custard, sprinkle the top with the brown sugar. Chill until needed & place under a hot grill until the sugar has caramelized.

EGG SET VANILLA CUSTARD

500ml whipping cream
1 vanilla pod
75g caster sugar
8 egg yolks
pinch nutmeg

Bring the cream up to a gently simmer with the seeds
from the vanilla pod. In a bowl, beat the eggs, sugar
& nutmeg, add the cream & mix well, pour through a
sieve into a baking tray. Bake for approx 30 minutes.

FRUIT FINGERS & DIPS

slices of
strawberries
apples
mango
pineapple
crème fraiche
cinnamon

In a small bowl dust the crème fraiche with the cinnamon,
place the slices of fruit around the dipping bowl.

RHUBARB & APPLE FANCY

4 digestive biscuits crumbled
stewed rhubarb
stewed apples
raisins
crème fraiche

In a dessert dish put 2 tablespoons of biscuits, a layer of crème fraiche, then fruit, repeat and top off with crème fraiche & raisins.

For a richer flavour melt 25g butter & pour over the crumbled biscuits.

Why not add vanilla to the crème fraiche?

HOT CHOCOLATE FUDGE
BANANA FONDUE

1 banana
1 bar cooking chocolate
50ml double cream
marshmallows

Slice a banana & place on a plate around a fondue bowl with the marshmallows. In a glass bowl melt the chocolate over simmering water, add the cream & fold in gently. Fill the fondue bowl with the melted chocolate fudge, serve with skewers for dipping & plenty of kitchen roll.

HIDE & SEEK FUDGE FONDUE

1 bar cooking chocolate
50ml double cream
mini marshmallows
strawberries
chunks of brownie cake

Melt the chocolate in a bowl over simmering water, add the cream & stir in gently. In a serving dish put the strawberries, marshmallows & brownie chunks, pour over the chocolate so that they are buried. Now seek!

BANANA CREAM WHIP

1 banana
pinch cinnamon
100ml double cream

In a blender put the banana & cream, blend until thick & smooth.

Serve in a glass & dust with cinnamon.

For a really sweet banana, caramelize in a frying pan with brown sugar before blending.

BANANA CHEESE WHIP

1 banana
100ml double cream
50g cream cheese
1 tbsp brown sugar
1 tbsp butter
1 tsp brown sugar
cinnamon

Gently melt the butter & sugar, add the sliced banana, cook until soft & caramelized. In a separate pan pour in the cream & warm through, stir in the cream cheese, cool & blend.

In a dish layer the caramelized banana & cream, finish off with a dusting of cinnamon.

YOGHURT CRUMBLE

fruit yoghurt
honey
oatmeal

Take a tumbler, drizzle the honey around the inside of the glass, layer the oatmeal, honey & yoghurt to the top.

PRUNE FOOL

1 tin prunes de-stoned
apricot yoghurt
oatmeal biscuits crushed
1 tbsp butter

Melt the butter & mix with the biscuits, blend the
prunes & in a dessert dish layer the biscuits, yoghurt
& prunes.

PEAR & PAPAYA CREAM

ripe pear
ripe papaya
100ml double cream
1 tsp brown sugar
½ juice of lemon

Peel the fruit & roughly chop, place in the blender & add the cream & lemon juice. Blend until smooth & thick, put into dessert dishes, sprinkle with brown sugar & chill.

CARAMELIZED FRUIT

wedges of orange
mango
pineapple
banana
2 tsp brown sugar
2 tbsp honey
2 tsp brown sugar
½ carton crème fraiche

Sprinkle the fruit wedges with the sugar & place in a hot non-stick pan & caramelize. Leave to one side, return the pan to the heat & add the honey, heat & pour over the fruit. Allow to cool before serving & serve with the crème fraiche dip.

LIME MANGO PEACH CREAM

mango slices
peach slices
100ml double cream whipped
1lime ½ squeezed / juiced
2 tbsp sugar

Whip the double cream with the lime & sugar, until firm peaks. Puree the mango & peach. In a ramekin, place a slice of lime top with cream & fruit puree, repeat & chill until served.